This book was transcribed from one of the thousands of sermons of Bill Vincent. Please realize this as you read this book. Thanks for your purchase and support.

Supernatural Power

Bill Vincent

Published by RWG Publishing, 2021.

While every precaution has been taken in the preparation of this book, the publisher assumes no responsibility for errors or omissions, or for damages resulting from the use of the information contained herein.

SUPERNATURAL POWER

First edition. October 22, 2021.

Copyright © 2021 Bill Vincent.

Written by Bill Vincent.

Also by Bill Vincent

Building a Prototype Church: Divine Strategies Released
Experience God's Love: By Revival Waves of Glory School of the Supernatural
Glory: Expanding God's Presence
Glory: Increasing God's Presence
Glory: Kingdom Presence of God
Glory: Pursuing God's Presence
Glory: Revival Presence of God
Rapture Revelations: Jesus Is Coming
The Prototype Church: Heaven's Strategies for Today's Church
The Secret Place of God's Power
Transitioning Into a Prototype Church: New Church Arising
Spiritual Warfare Made Simple
Aligning With God's Promises
A Closer Relationship With God
Armed for Battle: Spiritual Warfare Battle Commands
Breakthrough of Spiritual Strongholds
Desperate for God's Presence: Understanding Supernatural Atmospheres
Destroying the Jezebel Spirit: How to Overcome the Spirit Before It Destroys You!
Discerning Your Call of God
Glory: Expanding God's Presence: Discover How to Manifest God's Glory

Glory: Kingdom Presence Of God: Secrets to Becoming Ambassadors of Christ
Satan's Open Doors: Access Denied
Spiritual Warfare: The Complete Collection
The War for Spiritual Battles: Identify Satan's Strategies
Understanding Heaven's Court System: Explosive Life Changing Secrets
A Godly Shaking: Don't Create Waves
Faith: A Connection of God's Power
Global Warning: Prophetic Details Revealed
Overcoming Obstacles
Spiritual Leadership: Kingdom Foundation Principles
Glory: Revival Presence of God: Discover How to Release Revival Glory
Increasing Your Prophetic Gift: Developing a Pure Prophetic Flow
Millions of Churches: Why Is the World Going to Hell?
The Supernatural Realm: Discover Heaven's Secrets
The Unsearchable Riches of Christ: Chosen to be Sons of God
Deep Hunger: God Will Change Your Appetite Toward Him
Defeating the Demonic Realm
Glory: Increasing God's Presence: Discover New Waves of God's Glory
Growing In the Prophetic: Developing a Prophetic Voice
Healing After Divorce: Grace, Mercy and Remarriage
Love is Waiting
Awakening of Miracles: Personal Testimonies of God's Healing Power
Deception and Consequences Revealed: You Shall Know the Truth and the Truth Shall Set You Free
Overcoming the Power of Lust
Are You a Follower of Christ: Discover True Salvation
Cover Up and Save Yourself: Revealing Sexy is Not Sexy
Heaven's Court System: Bringing Justice for All
The Angry Fighter's Story: Harness the Fire Within
The Wrestler: The Pursuit of a Dream

Beginning the Courts of Heaven: Understanding the Basics
Breaking Curses: Legal Rights in the Courts of Heaven
Writing and Publishing a Book: Secrets of a Christian Author
How to Write a Book: Step by Step Guide
The Anointing: Fresh Oil of God's Presence
Spiritual Leadership: Kingdom Foundation Principles Second Edition
The Courts of Heaven: How to Present Your Case
The Jezebel Spirit: Tactics of Jezebel's Control
Heaven's Angels: The Nature and Ranking of Angels
Don't Know What to Do?: Discover Promotion in the Wilderness
Word of the Lord: Prophetic Word for 2020
The Coronavirus Prophecy
Increase Your Anointing: Discover the Supernatural
Apostolic Breakthrough: Birthing God's Purposes
The Healing Power of God: Releasing the Power of the Holy Spirit
The Secret Place of God's Power: Revelations of God's Word
The Rapture: Details of the Second Coming of Christ
Increase of Revelation and Restoration: Reveal, Recover & Restore
Leadership vs Management
Restoration of the Soul: The Presence of God Changes Everything
Building a Prototype Church: The Church is in a Season of Profound of Change
Keys to Receiving Your Miracle: Miracles Happen Today
The Resurrection Power of God: Great Exploits of God
Transitioning to the Prototype Church: The Church is in a Season of Profound of Transition
Waves of Revival: Expect the Unexpected
The Stronghold of Jezebel: A True Story of a Man's Journey
Glory: Pursuing God's Presence: Revealing Secrets
Like a Mighty Rushing Wind
Steps to Revival
Supernatural Power

Watch for more at https://revivalwavesofgloryministries.com/.

Supernatural Power

We know that a lot of it is held up in the realm of the Spirit. So, we want to bring it down. And all these different things that I'm talking about have to do with that realm of the supernatural, where God is where he is doing things, and there's so much manifesting that we've we're getting ready to tap into, and we're getting ready to receive. And I thank God for the gifts of the Spirit, I thank God for the gifts of prophecy and the nine gifts of the Holy Spirit. But I believe that there's even another realm, another step beyond just the gifts of the Holy Spirit. And because it falls in, it might be connected to those gifts. But it's just a whole other realm of the supernatural. And what I mean by this is, whenever God shows up, that's His Glory. When he shows up and you'll begin to feel his presence, and things begin to manifest like gold dust and things, that's just signs that he's here. And when he shows up, I want you to know that when he shows up, things begin to happen. And things that you normally would have to do, you don't have to do in the glory. And what I mean by that is, we pray for one another and do all these different things. Sometimes in the presence of God, people just start getting healed. People just start getting set free. Why? Because it's his glory, sickness, and sin and those things don't have any place in the glory. Because it's Kingdom earth as it is in heaven, as it isn't heaven.

How many want that as it is in heaven? In Your Life. There's no sickness in heaven, there's freedom in heaven. The of the greatest examples I can use that I want to use is Daniel. Because Daniel, he did have supernatural. He did have supernatural power and abilities. I was pressing into God, and all of a sudden, it's like I begin to see tools. And I saw as being equipped. This is what I'm talking about tonight is being equipped. And some people want a whole Arsenal, they want the whole thing. I mean, they want that toolbelt so full, that it's ready to go. God even talked about having weapons of mass destruction. And what I mean, how many are sick and tired of being sick and tired, it's time for the enemy to have mass destruction. When the enemy brings sickness about one of us, we're going to go get ten saved. And it's time for people to be getting saved, you can be set free and being delivered. So, Daniel, and he had three friends. And they are a representation of how the Lord is about to equip us. Because there is so much that they received that was beyond everyone else. And that's why I want us to, I want us to be able to be equipped beyond anything that we've ever seen, heard, or even understood. Are you ready for that? But understand when this comes, there's going to be a whole lot going on with it. You're gonna pay the price, the full price.

We're going to have an enjoyable time. But understand. Let's go to Daniel chapter one, verse seventeen. And this describes special abilities from heaven that were imparted to loyal men of God.

So, we got to be loyal to the Lord. That's a funny word. Oh boy, when I start getting caught on words, you know what happens next, another wave comes, and another wave comes, and another way of comes. But let's look at this Daniel chapter one, verse seventeen, it talks about that they had intelligence, intelligence, and every branch of literature and wisdom, Daniel even understood all kinds of dreams and visions. And I want you to understand the abilities that were given from the throne. How many want that impartation of the abilities beyond your own? I mean, it's just like, you just have intelligence beyond your intelligence. Right? I could say something. But I'm just gonna move on. I'm gonna give Johnny a free pass on that one. The Lord gave them inspiration, regulatory knowledge, and intelligence, in various matters of writing and literature. God is about to birth authors. That's one thing. God is speaking to me to author the books, author the books, author the books. Is this before or after I sleep? I mean, it's like, my plate is already full. You know how hard it is to establish a new ministry and get it going to the level that God's got us going in this past four months, and all these different things that I'm telling you, it's amazing that we're even where we're at. I mean, it is amazing because the enemy came in to try to destroy. That's what the Spirit was trying to do with destroying me. And I'm telling you that I had to come out fighting and I had to go ahead and let the accusations and all the things go with it. And that's what the church does sometimes whenever they don't understand some of what's going on. They just begin to lash out. And we need to understand that in this time, we need the gifts we need the supernatural impartation from heaven. And I don't care how young you are, or how not young you are. God has impartation he wants to give to you the Lord gave them, and I want you to know the Lord quicken in their specific skills. How long? How many have specific skills? I'm not talking about just your you know that between cooking and not cooking. I can say something with that, but I'm not going to either.

I'm gonna go ahead and say something, but I'm not going to say who it was in the past four months. A couple of times someone's tried to cook they've cooked very well when it's in the oven. Or the microwave you know? Or a little bit of stovetop but when it comes to the grease and the fire, you know the real getting things heated up. The first time they tried to get the fried chicken. That was a disaster. That chicken was not fit to eat, till the last piece. They decide at 7:30, 8 p.m. They're gonna have fried chicken for dinner. How many know that's gonna be one late dinner. And you know there's something wrong with that whenever they say how do you do it. And so, but then Time goes by, and I don't remember what they were going to fry. But all I know is I had a pan of oil full blast heat on that oil. Well, the pan catches on fire. I grabbed that pan flaming all burning my hairs finally grown back, grow, you know, burn in my hairs right off my hands as I'm taking it to the sink. And then it goes all over the kitchen for a split second and goes away. And it left black marks everywhere. Praise God. The reason I'm telling you this story is because it's making you laugh.

But at the same time, I'm talking about specific skills. It's just like God can impart something in you that you can't do. You can't do it and all of a sudden, it's like God has imparted into you to do something you've never done before, it would be like they would be able to walk in there and fry a whole chicken. without, you know, having to cut it and everything, they'd be able to cut it and fry it because of the impartation that would take place. So how many would like to have something in an area that gives them the Holy Spirit gives them what God gives you to be able to do something you've never done before. Just to sit down and begin to write, sit down, and begin to publish and do things and have a revelation that's coming straight from the throne because it is a revelation. This is the way it's gonna happen. It's gonna happen to those who are ready to receive whatever he has. Daniel was notable, gifted with the supernatural perception of dreams and visions. How many know we need to understand the dreams and visions even today? How many have ever had a dream and you tell everybody, and you get five, six different answers what they believe it means.

Oh, you were in a boat. That means you're in ministry. No, you were in a boat, which means you're trying to get away. You were in a boat, which means you're about to sink. How many know there's an interpretation, and there's an interpretation. Let me tell you something, I want my dreams interpreted by one Holy Spirit. I don't want an interpretation by you know, all these different people. And I have been in ministry long enough to see that a lot of people don't know what they're talking about. That I love it when they say I read it in a book that this means this. Was it this book? Was it this book? Did it line up with this book? Because if it didn't, I wouldn't want to hear what that book has to say. Oh, Jesus, aren't you getting quiet. Okay, let's go on. The Lord was specific, was a specific impartation there was a specific impartation from God that empowered them to excel, and they excelled in wisdom. They excelled with, like, understanding beyond our knowledge, how many what that so consumed by God that God excels you. Some of us need an accelerator. I mean, we read the word and we're like, what's that mean? Why is that there? Why is that there? What is this for? Now all of a sudden, when God brings impartation, it's like, somebody just turned a light on. Some of you need a light turned on. The Lord is bestowed by spiritual transference, the blessing of unique knowledge, exceptional capacity in literature, and all of the written work. I'm telling you, it's like supernatural knowledge to be able to write things. And I have actually, there have been so many times where I need a sermon so quick because of time because you're about to have some things happen. And I need to have a sermon quick. And I'll go in there and just begin to type and within an hour, you know, I can have 20 to 30 pages if this comes straight from the throne of God. And that's without looking up a scripture or anything. It's the revelation from the throne. he gives me the Scripture. Hum on, it's time for us to understand that when God says turn to Isaiah, guess what, there's something in Isaiah. And we need to understand, I don't know about you, but I don't want to just hear another sermon about faith. If it's not something right now. I don't want to hear something going on in the area of finances. Unless there's a revelation for right now.

I know you're excited but calm down. This pattern will also be followed. On this day, when the Lord discovers devoted hearts of obedience, and loyalty. You know why God has you jump through the same hoops over and over and over again a lot of times because of obedience. He was to see if you're gonna do it. Don't you hate those hoops? Don't you hate jumping through them repeatedly? And some of you need to be honest. Why do we get to do this again, there are vast warehouses? Listen to me vast storehouses of regulatory insight, and supernatural knowledge involving the scriptures, creation, science, arts, many other subjects that will be entrusted to saints who follow the model established by Daniel and his three friends. Well, we are loyal to the Lord. When we are obedient to what the Lord wants us to do, he will give us an understanding of things. Say, one of the things we need to understand he'll give you an understanding of science that you never had. I wasn't that good at science because I hated it. But understand, when it came to God, he began to let me know that he upholds all things in his hand. All things in his hand. And so, whenever I pray for somebody, and they got a tumor, it's already in God's hands, he can dissolve that tumor, just as fast as it got there. Or faster than it got there. God can do anything when it comes to elements, he can bring increase, he can bring decrease, how long. And I also understand that Jesus can walk on water was because God, I believe, can even change the molecules. For that time to make things happen. God can change things in the area of wind. He can cause the seas to part. So, we need to understand our little world. We didn't understand he can do it. You say what can he do? Whatever you want him to do anything above what you can ask her to think he can do. And I believe there's an impartation of these things that are about to come to where we're going to understand it this science has, has tried, and tried and tried to disprove the Bible. But guess what, they haven't been able to do it. Do you know why? Because they'll never be able to never, everybody tried to get the codes out the codes, there are codes in here, you know, there was one, one interpretation. You actually can get it in India, it's a software called the Bible code. And you can get it, she just had to wait two or three months to get it. And it cost. You know, I don't remember how much.

But I remember I was with somebody, and you can believe it or not believe it. They had the software, and they typed in their name. They typed in their name, first, middle, and last name. And they were able to find using words from the Bible, under certain numbers of the words. It talked about the very ministry; they were called to come in straight from this book. Do you say you don't believe it? You don't know if it's right. Now I understand the Holy Spirit's the one that wrote this.

And the prophetic word is from this word. So, understand there's an interpretation we haven't even discovered yet. Now I understand some people try to use this to understand the end of the world. And guess what, they're just messing it up. because nobody's going to know the time to the season but some signs will come. And we need to understand that. But at the same time, I'm just saying there's so much yet to be discovered. So much that's yet to be found out. And also, there is so much in you have abilities that you don't even know you have. Understand, understand. I used to be a bashful young man, who was shy, who did not under did not do good at school for several years because of my rebellion.

And God called me out of that place and to ministry, to be able to understand things that I understand. And he has done miracles. He's done science, he's done wonders. He's given me revelations. And he's wanting me to write all these books and different things. I've authored some books. The last ministry ended up obtaining all those things. Praise God. That's okay. Because God's gonna give me new, Praise God. A bit of advice to everyone, be careful. Even in ministry, you can't trust some people, sometimes, because sometimes they can take it right for Monday. There's a prophetic standard God's raising. How many believe that? A prophetic standard? Now understand, I'm still talking about Daniel and his three friends. Young men, these young men provide a prophetic standard for spiritually strong, who know their God and carry out great exploits. See, we need to know our God and carry out great exploits. How many believe that. See, if we don't walk in power, we're no different than any other religion. They gather together. They have their meeting, they go home. And we gather together and have our meeting to go home. And now that happens, we're no different than any religion. Lord, Jesus. How many want to get away from that? How many want to walk in power and great exploits? I don't want to just hear the word only. But I want to be a doer. I want us to be a doer. a doer of the word? Are you ready for the doer? Do you want to be a doer? It's getting hot up here. Do you? Do you? Do you want to be a doer of the word? Or do you want to be here only? Do you want to have revelation not just from some other man's revelation, but revelation from heaven? He says, well, you know, I'm still wet behind ears. I'm not called to be an apostle. I'm not called to be a prophet. you're called to be a child of God. And you've got an inheritance being a king's kid. Jesus is the King. And through that inheritance, you already have much your call to I don't care if you're not called to fivefold. Do you like it? People are going to be intimate with the Lord and know how to engage the heavenly realm. How many believe that? We're going to know how to engage the heavenly realm. You know you got to engage the heavenly realm. Sometimes we're just Like I'm supposed to come here. It's not a puppy. We're expecting heaven to come like, It's not a puppy. You've got to breakthrough. Sometimes you got to worship for a while. And we put God on I keep preaching this way. And I keep saying this over and over and over again. And I repeat myself because guess what, we need to hear it.

We put God on this 15-minute timer. God, I'm gonna give you 15 minutes you show up? We're gonna have an enjoyable time. Oh, I can feel him. Oh, yes. Got to go. Yes, we're gonna have revival soon, with that kind of attitude. I like a song that I play every once in a while. It's I pray till Jesus comes. How many want to pray till Jesus comes? You say that's a long time. Well, it's time for us to pray to Jesus police officers. There's time for us to press in. Like, like we have to. Because that's what we do. By the looks of this world, we need to pray. By the looks of the church, we need to pray. Is the church sick and tired over and over again? People afflicted people have to take medications. You know, sometimes I have seen on this, you know, the signs that we have at the churches, they put those cute little sayings on, and everyone's all seen a church who believes in miracles, and they'll have a have it on the sign. And there's nothing wrong with this, but they'll say handicap entrance side. Do you know you know? And, you know, I want to say in the days ahead to where we have a whole lot of miracles taking place in the everyday church. it's time for that. And God even said that Springfield is one of those cities it's going to be recognized for the lame being healed. How many want to see the Civic Center pitfall? How many you want to see people's capacity like it is for a basketball game. How many want to see the capacity overwhelming, where people can't even get in the door, and they're being healed right here on Ninth Street and Fifth Street and all these streets. gets around here, just trying to get into a giant stadium to hear what God is doing. That's what's about to take place. God's about to hit this city so strong, there won't be room enough for the people. Remember, I'm not just saying, I'm prophesied what God's saying.

There will be people who apprehend insight from the throne room. respond to the invitation, come up here. See, there's a door standing open in heaven that was prophesied in the book of revelations, Chapter Four. They said, there's a door standing open in heaven saying, there was a sound of a voice that came from there, that said, Come up here. That door is still standing open. There's nowhere in Scripture that says it shut. And I believe that there's that door at an invitation has been taken place that's even taking place right now. That saying, Come up here. There's an invitation for insight, an invitation for revelation. You're not going to get revelation by just having it here, you have to have it from the supernatural. You can't just get revelation from all the books. I used to have a preacher we always had; we were all being trained at the same time. So, we had a group of preachers being trained. And this one preacher, he walked up there, and he'd have a stack of books, and he just take them all, bounces them all on the pulpit. And he has, you know, the Strong's and, you know, Thompson chain, and also a couple of other books that just were good, and he'd have a pile of books, you know, and he'd be talking for a while, and then he read from this book, and then he talked, and it was good. It was good. But there was nothing fresh. Some of those revelations are hundreds of years old. Oh, Jesus. And I want you to know that I thank God for those books, and they're very useful. And we can use it for interpreting the scripture in some ways but understand that's not the throne zone. That's not the throne room experience. That's not us going to heaven say responding to the come up here. A few years ago, during a prophetic experience, the Lord especially stated to me two scriptures, and I've used these a few times in my preaching, Daniel 1:17, and Ephesians 1:17. God said these are parallel, parallel, with the same promise from different timeframes. Let's go ahead and look at them.

Thank you, Lord Jesus. You just have a big Bible. Now this Bible that shuts every time you turn to a page, it's like, stay open. Okay? Ephesians 1:17. It says that the God of our Lord Jesus Christ, the Father of glory, may give unto you the spirit of wisdom, and Revelation, and the knowledge of Him. Now, let's go back to Daniel, Now I want you to understand, God speaks, and we need to listen. So many times, people are a body of Christ. It's not easy to listen to God and make sermons. Why? Because you're completely trusting in him. So, I remember the first couple of times God would give me a sermon, I mean from the throne, throne, and he would give me a sermon, and it'd be like a page long. And I'm like, God, that's not enough. I need more. And I tried to study out and add to it, you know, I'm gonna get an interpretation, I'm gonna get definitions, I'm gonna get all those things put together at the end of it. And then what I find out is I preach, and I preach for an hour or two. With that one page. Why? It's what you gave me. It's all I needed. he knows what to give. Let's look at Daniel 117. It says this. As for these children, God gave them knowledge, and the skill in all learning and wisdom, and Daniel had understanding and all visions and dreams. Look at this. There is a parallel. These are parallel passages stating the same promise from different timeframes. One is from the old one is from the new, Old Covenant, New Covenant. The other is expressed in a new covenant recording for all generations. See so many people I have had this over and over and over again. People more or less argue with me saying that's for the Old Covenant. That's not for us. This is in the new and the old. It is for us to have a divine revelation; how do you want it? How many want divine revelation from heaven? Do you need it, we all need it?

SUPERNATURAL POWER   11

I've used this illustration before I'm on my head and use it again, Maria Woodworth Etter had meetings, and they would be caught up in an experience revelation. And they have experienced this revelation as a whole congregation, the whole body of Christ in their church and their services would experience a revelation at the same time, they would be caught up in Revelation into where some of them would begin to see the country they were called to and begin to even speak the language. And it's been documented. How many would like that to happen in your church? It's like, all of a sudden, they start speaking various places have, you know, from Africans speak some Chinese and just have an understanding they just came straight from the throne. Imagine how fast we could be anointed and sent. You know, some are called Some are sent, some just got up and went. I don't want to just get up and go, I want God to send me

it is the Father's good pleasure to reveal to us the kingdom. It is his good pleasure to reveal to us the kingdom and perform awesome deeds that only he can achieve. I don't know about you, but I want to get out of the ordinary into the extraordinary. I want to get into the things that nobody's gonna be able to deny. There'll be like, whoa, how'd that happen? Listen to me, it was a small thing for God to rejuvenate the body of Sarah, it was a small thing for him to rejuvenate a body to be able to give birth to children. a small thing. When I'm talking about supernatural power, I'm talking about abilities that are beyond what you can even imagine being able to do and see in the realm of the Spirit beyond what you could ever imagine. What I mean is there's gonna be times people are gonna be able to prophesy The word of the Lord and be able to see inside of people's bodies to such a degree that they're going to know exactly what's wrong with the bloodline, what's going on with the organs, what's going on in the area of sugar, whatever, they're going to know it and they're going to know the diagnosis. Why? Because it's going to be a word of knowledge with greater power. Why? Because it's a new realm of Revelation. Oh, The Lord is more than able to equip us to access the unfathomable treasures hidden in heaven.

We can find treasures in heaven that are been hidden since the foundation of the world. Apostle Paul found some of these treasures. And look how many years they were hidden before he found them. Don't you think it's about time we start finding some hidden treasures? Now I used to be a real history buff when it comes to God, not the history of everything else. Just godly history, revivals, and different things. And we are right now if history repeats itself. This season, we're in between 2005 to 2025 is an open heaven Season Two where we're going to be in to see and experience things beyond anything we've ever experienced. And it's a new launch of the supernatural Much like the olden Azusa Street Revival, part of the inheritance of that is getting ready to repeat itself. It's already been prophesied come up, and we are coming into greater things. I'm not talking about a false revival that has come and gone. I'm talking about real revival. We're real people are being saved. Real miracles are taking place. Real people are given total Glory to the Lord. And it's gonna come from some strange places. Johnny will go home with anyone that wants to take her home.

One night with Johnny will change your life forever. get you out of that comfort zone? Mostly Yes. What? Do you mean another lot of people? No, they're not laughing at me. No, there. There's a biblical state of holy laughter. Even God left in the Bible. They're not laughing at me. They're laughing because of the anointing because of the presence of God, it begins to break things out. It's uncontrollable, and even happens a lot of times where I'm trying to preach serious sermons. And it's not I mean, this is nothing. He should have been some of the past services. This is very minor. I've been in services where people paid to, so we won't go there.

Thank you, so anything can happen in any service? Yes, nursing home, that's where it was. I'm not talking about everyday church. But there's also I mean, there are even times where people start manifesting devils. So there, anything can happen. So, let's go ahead and continue for a minute. Even now, individuals are engaging the regulatory realm. And what I mean by this is not just a little bit of understanding a little bit of wisdom, but beyond anything, you can imagine. I'm talking about so much to where you can hardly even contain it. It's like a bubbling up out of you. Revelation. I'm telling you, there are a couple of people over the last decade when they released their books, it was life-changing. You read them, and it's like, wow, this is awesome. Now, there's not enough of those. There's a whole lot of books. There's not enough revelation in those books. And what I mean is, we're coming into a day, right now that there's going to be heavenly downloads. Continuous download, too many limitations are being put out there. Too many limitations and boundaries, this has to be in this way. We have to have it in this form. What we've done is we box God in, you can't move beyond these perimeters. Guess what? It's time for God to go ahead and start spitting on eyes again. his time if it's gonna cause miracles, let it cause miracles. I don't know about you, but if I need to see, you can spit. I've got ten preachers' spit on me if they think it's God.

If they believe it's God, why? Because I don't want to limit what God can do. He can do it. However, he wants to what if God told us to, we're supposed to dip seven times, it's biblical. And we're gonna step into some of these things in the days ahead. And we need to be very careful not to limit what God's gonna do in the days ahead. Even now, there these individuals are engaging, that there's even something that in the physic realm, physics, quantum physics, light, sound, or supernatural spiritual colors that are coming for us, come up. There's something about that. Now, I understand when I see people, sometimes I'll look at a person, I'll see red. Now with God, it's an interpretation that they have cancer. And I prophesied that many, many times. And people have been healed many, many, many times. And I'm telling you, it's just like God just comes on the scene. When I say that color. Why? Because he's using the color. Now that's not with every person who sees in the spirit.

That's just the way God has taught me. The visitation of the apostle John to the throne. Understand, was both visual and audible. Not only did he see things, but he also heard how many want to have that type of visitation to where you not only hear, but you also see. There are too many of us that are doubting there's too many of the body of Christ that doubt what God can do. And we doubt things and we question things. Because we haven't seen or heard. It's time for us to have experiences. Don't you want to have experiences where you can hardly contain yourself? Oh, that had to be real. I want to be blown away. Ordinary churches aren't blowing me away, I want to be blown away. Get ready, things are about to burst. Things are about to burst. Everything's gonna be okay. Remember, that's nice. The song God said was gonna be the theme of this ministry for a while. And guess what he just said to me, this week, I just realized this. I just remember, he said, the song that said it's all going to be okay. is not going to be needing to be the song for you. By March, because March is the bursting forth. So, in other words, we're not going to need that it's going to be okay, it's going to be okay. Because we're going to know it's okay. Because look out how many want to have a lookout. Now, his experience talking about john had awesome lights, sounds vibrant colors surrounding the Lord Sea of dominion and victory. I gave a sermon many years ago, about the sound of glory. You know those sound waves in your body, and the sound waves have to respond to the word.

Oh, you need to understand this. When we prophesy and decree a thing, it's going to be established because of the sound that is released, the body must respond. And I'm telling you, there's a sound that's about to come forth in the heavenly. There's open heaven that is about to take place. And I'm telling you, there's going to be greater miracles and healings across a decade that we've never experienced before. And I'm talking about it's going to be easy to have miracles in the local church, it's time for that. I don't know about you. But it's upsetting. For us to have some guy from an international ministry show up to our city to have a little tickle to get a little excited. And then it goes home where we all die. I don't know about you, but the church has been dead too long. And I'm including myself in the boat. Why? Because of miracle signs and wonders, there are a whole lot more miracles, signs, and wonders yet needed to be. Many people still need to have miracles. Too many people still need to have signs and wonders do many people need to be awakened? So however much I've had been still not enough.

. People being awakened. And understanding science and physics and elements of creation are not going to be super-geniuses. or scientific minds. They're going to be anointed men and women of God. Don't you want that? Don't you want us to be an anointed man or woman of God to where it's not about me? It's about him. And I want you to know, I call myself this sometimes every once in a while, whenever I begin to have such revelation, such knowledge. I begin to go to the Lord and say I made you say What's wrong? Why would you do that? Because I don't want my smarts. I want his smarts. I'm like, God, I don't I'm stupid before you I am ignorant before you, I am filthy before you. I want you to redeem me, I want you to cleanse me, and I want you to anoint me, I can't do anything without you. I can't preach the Word of God without you. I can't talk to somebody about God without you. I can't lay hands on a person without you. I cannot walk and the anointing of miracles, signs, and wonders without you. I need you. And I'm telling you that's why I want to break free from that over and over and over again and put my flesh down because it needs to be put down. too many of us get proud and arrogant when we start tapping in because we're anointed now guess what? We're nobody. I love that whenever I was young, and the Lord God began to say to me over and over again. My son I've called you you're gonna be a mighty man of God. You're anointed. You're gonna be Somebody, and you're going to do wonderful things, and you're gonna have miracles, signs, and wonders. And I'd hear that over and over and over again. And then I start ministering, I start preaching and God begins to minister through me. And then all of a sudden, I received a word saying, You're nobody. You're nothing without me. You tap into me, and I cause you to be great. That's awesome. That's an awesome revelation for us to have. We all need it, that's a good pastors conference to have. For us all to be put in our place. It's all about me. No, it's not. It's all about him. It's all about building my kingdom. No, it's not. It's about building his kingdom. I'm always right. And you're always wrong. No, he's always right. It's not whether I'm right. You're right. It's about him being right. I don't know about you. But it's, but we now understand people sometimes don't have a revelation. That's why we need this. We need these gifts. We need this anointed; we need this ability. We need God to get our arsenal ready. And how many know the devil is real? We need to deal with it swiftly. I don't know about you, but I'm tired of being on defense. I want to be on offense. I want to bring the battle to the enemy, go into the bad neck of the woods and bring them out of there. Good. People say good people have praise, that that will be like what are they going to do next? Instead of worrying about what he's gonna do next, we have. We have all the angels behind us. We have God who is omnipresent everywhere at all times, we should be victory after victory after victory. Just what Jesus did on the cross has broken everything for us. Broken at wide open for us with victories already been won. I'm still on the last page. Are you ready?

Some of you should have been in that over two years a revival we were in night after night, week after week. There will be times when people as I was preaching would just fall out of their seats and I just continue. There were times I preach, and I walk down the aisle and they just begin to fall in the aisles. You got to get used to it after a while. And by the end of the revival is like oh, that's just them. I'll just step over them and continue preaching. We had a lot of pile-ups.

Yes, we had those too. We had a very narrow hallway. People trying to leave the service. And sometimes they had to walk over people because they were piling up on the exit. There were times we let out the service at 10 o'clock and it took till 11:30 to get them out the door. It's like Why? Because they were drunk in the spirit. But look back at the disciples in the book of Acts. They act like drunkards. They know what the Bible says they look like an actor like drunk people thought they were drunk they were just here with the power of God we as a church need that well I don't know we don't need all that silly this, we need something more, don't we? If we don't have miracles taking place in our church, we need something different, somebody changed the format or something. Somebody gets a new get a new wineskin on or something we need something new, something fresh. If God's gonna move. And I'm telling you he is about to move.

The most ordinary Christians who are tapping into the heart of God desiring to release supernatural gifts and abilities of his mind is what we're doing. We're released in the supernatural of his mind. God is all-knowing. He knows everything. And every pickle we get into he's gonna know the way out. That's another man. I was preaching about soaking in God's presence. And I had some religion come against me because of this. Here's what I said. I said I want God to pick on me

and what I mean by You know, if you've ever made pickles, they have to marinate. I want to marinate in this presence. I want to soak until I'm started to smell, taste just like him. So, I said pickle me and people got all upset with me. I even had one board member say, you're gonna lose salary on that one. They said I was gonna lose some salary on that one. I was like, you take much more, I have nothing. Praise the Lord. I'll release them and blast them in. What I loved was, they got on me for stuff like that. Then David Herzog came. And I was cleansed of all bad doing because he could, he said some things that kind of got on the fence line. With his tippy toes, I'd repeat them. But you know, I don't want to, but anyway. But he, you know, and it was he was proper, but it was just, he goes out on the edge and then come back, go out on the edge, and then come back. And that one board member, she started looking at me. Like I knew it. I never met him before that day. holiday. All right, let's go. Much is going to be spoken. And written in the coming days involving the dimension of our heritage. We have a heritage, our heritage,

I'm not just talking about, you know, we have a heritage here on Earth. I'm talking about the heritage of heavenly heritage. We have a heavenly heritage. I'm a king's kid. Oh, I have an inheritance.

And it's a heavenly inheritance, and I want my inheritance. Now. I don't want to wait till I die. Back when I minister to the nursing homes, they always love the song I'll fly away. And that's a good song. It is. One time I preach the sermon after singing that song and preaching the sermon on, but I want it before I fly. I want to before I fly, I'll fly away. But I want some heaven right now. I want some heaven before I die. I want to get to heaven and say, whoa, Because God even said in the simplicity of his prayer, life Kingdom earth as it is in heaven. I want heaven right here, it's time to have heaven. God gave me a promise as a young man of God. I was a young man of God. I was 17 years old. And I received a prophetic word about being called to preach and all these different things that God said, I'm going to give you heaven on earth. I was expecting one thing and he made another. how many? No, he always means something naughty. And I'm telling you it is so awesome to have a heavenly realm right here in our midst, over and over and over again. And we're just getting started, we're about to see the greatest things we've ever seen in our life. I'm talking about when people walk in the service, they're going to be getting out of wheelchairs. Did you hear me? They're wheeling in and walking in? Will an end and check your chair at the door? Instead, we try to make room for him. Move some chairs and what about getting them healed before they got to come up the steps?

I remember when I was in a service one time and the minister was running out of room. The Pat place was packed and there were three wheelchairs was coming out of this van they go we don't have room for three wheelchairs. They go we're gonna have to carry Oh man. I said I'm in a wheelchair. And the preacher was walking by, and he goes, are we gonna do that? Why don't we just get them healed right here? Now, remember, you got a whole packed house inside. Ready for church. Well, we're all out on the sidewalk. Praise God. I'll catch you because I'm the

Usher type of guy out there and he's praying for him. He says rise and walk. I'm like you're not done yet. I was still stuck in some of that old time. Religion, I thought you got to keep doing it till it's done. He said, leave them here that come in when they're ready.

I was like that was nice. And he said, don't look back. I was like, yes, so I started walking in the service and I was trying to do my peripheral from a long distance. Try and couldn't see him. Good thing I might have turned into that pillar of salt, I don't know. But I go in the service. And as soon as I got in there, I felt this heat come up behind me. It was a hot body, it was them. All three of them walked into that service. All three of them. And two of them had been crippled for over 20 years, never walked. The other one had rheumatoid arthritis and could watch sometimes, but she was not just having a tough time she was having an enjoyable time. And I'm telling you the service started I'm like, come home, talk about it. Get the testimony out there, let a stir everybody up, let's go. And he never said a word. And all of a sudden, these three were swaying in the Spirit. He didn't say a word. And it went the service went three hours, four hours. And by the last bit of the service, people begin to recognize who they were. And that's when the lights started going on. Because they knew their light. Sister, wait a minute you are standing, they didn't know how to get healed, they got healed, they looked healthier. They weren't just able to walk. They weren't just getting, oh, I can walk, I can walk, Praise the Lord. They were like, I can walk. I can walk. Hello about you. But I believe parts of the interpretation of the Scripture have been taken away, because it's not just many times, whenever God heals, he makes whole, it's not just being healed. I don't want to just get a little healing I want to be made Oh, I believe that we're able to do the work that Jesus did. And greater works than these. Now I understand. There were other times people are willing into the service. And that preacher was like, well find a place for him. I was like, we're supposed to do this every week. And one time he was preaching a sermon, and that's when I light went on. Thank God for those lights.

And he was preaching and all of a sudden, he said, there's times I see God doing things. And when I see him doing it, I have all confidence. There are other times I don't see him doing it. And I have to leap of faith. But he goes when I see it. I just say I don't care what people think people say. And that just happens easily because I saw it. And I began to understand that Jesus walked in did what he saw the father do, get ready to do only what you see the father do. But understand when you start doing what the father does, and they start walking. The people that you don't see are going to start walking by faith because of the others that got healed. Testimony begins to heal, get another one heals another testimony, then another one gets healed. And it begins to trickle out to the service. I remember one time I was praying; I was at a revival; I was on the ministry team. And I pray for a few people and my line was long, it was three people.

So, I'll spend a lot of time on the first one. And out of spending a lot of time and all of a sudden you know they begin to get hit with the power a little bit and they go, and they get set free or something and I pray for the next one, they start feeling better, and they started being set free to some and now pray for the third one. And they get hit got hit with the glory. I mean, it was like, like thunderbolts come out. The next thing I knew, here's another ten people. They started getting out of their seats making their way to the line. Why? Because they started seeing God move. And more. More people started coming, the more people started getting healed. And during that week, people that had metal in their neck were able to move their neck, people that couldn't walk was walking people that couldn't see one guy in the service that I prayed for, and a dozen other team members prayed for, but it doesn't matter. Jesus is the one that did it. He didn't even have an eyeball and he could see. He had a little wiggle thing. I don't know what to call a whale thing but it's the thing that connects to the eyeball. That's all I had. And he sees clear as a day. He knew color he knew everything was the handover as I look out how many want one of those, I know items.

What I mean by that God's gonna give you extraordinary gifts, special talents, special abilities, smith Wigglesworth, sometimes we would say, and so on the certain role in the purple dress being healed of this right now in Jesus' name. How many want that? You can't see in the natural, but you know that there, you have a detail of color, you have a detail of the person that they're female, I can have words of knowledge. But guess what, even here, I can see you. What about the stadium when they're on the fourth row of the, you know, the fifth level, get ready? I'm still on the last page. Much is going to be spoken and written. But also, like Einstein, there is going to be such a supernatural understanding of things. But understand he was so under, he wanted to understand of creation. Einstein did. But understand. We have the creator that can give us revelation of creation. That's more than Einstein ever had. And I'm telling you, the creator's gonna give us revelation. And he's gonna give us a revelation that will flourish in the hearts of many. But guess what? God's looking to and from across the Earth right now, looking for his chosen people who are willing, who are willing to pay the price, who are sick and tired of the church being dead? Who wants to be that one that's going to stand out a little bit, that's gonna have to take a leap of faith than mine?

Now, my pastor one time, here's what he said. He said I would rather try to do something great for God and fail than not try to do anything at all. What if they don't get healed? Next, get prayer, again. Your prayer again gets prayer, keep getting prayer till something breaks. Another thing I have learned over these past five years, especially, is I am never going to stop growing in God. Hello, I used to be a prophetic minister who prophesied the Word of God. And I released a word of the LORD and, and I would administer one on one over and over and over again, and praise God for that. But that's all I did. And then all of a sudden, people started getting healed, why? Because I was hungry. I wanted to see people healed.

And then all of a sudden, some things started happening in the realm of glory and presence and, and then signs and wonders, I don't want to stop there. Until I get to a place of everybody is being healed, everybody has been set free, everybody to be delivered. And the entire city being changed the entire region being changed at every, every place in the earth has an interpretation and understanding of what God's glory is. I don't want to stop growing, sometimes we keep putting periods behind us. Oh, that's my calling. I'm done. Guess what I'm not done. I'm gonna I want to do the work that Jesus did. And greater works. Greater. See, we all preach about doing the greater works when we haven't done the works. Oh, Jesus. We have access to the spiritual books of heaven. That will be granted. And when I said spiritual books of heaven, they haven't been written yet. You say, oh, some great man has to, Betty hen has to author those books, what about some housewife that has visitation and gets a revelation. And somebody reads that revelation, and they get a revelation because hey, learn they can get revelation. I don't know about you. But I don't care where the revelation comes from. I'll listen to a donkey if he's got it, let the rocks cry out. I don't care. I'm not going to limit it has to be by boat. No, I don't believe so. God says we're to equip the saints, for the work of the ministry, to the edifying of the body of Christ. Oh, Jesus, I knew that I knew that you get excited. I've been in churches sometimes and I start preaching this to pastors. fivefold ministry is going to be restored and it is, and you know the apostles and prophets are the foundation of the church. That's what the Bible is to talk about. That's been the foundation of the church. So, understand. A lot of the pastors are the ones ruling the church. Things are going to shift in the days ahead. Now the pastors are supposed to love the flock, guess what they're trying to do the apostolate work from a position that they are not able to love the flock. We need that pastor, but we need them to do, and some pastors get nervous when I start preaching that Why? Because they start thinking, what's gonna happen in my salary? If we get it right, in the days ahead, we're all going to have enough.

There's enough for us all to get fat and giggly. That's why you're gonna walk a lot. I can't wait till it warms up, those four Mile walks. I don't want to do it at all when it's cold. Those I have to walk last night. I had the two teeth pulled yesterday morning. Then I come here, I do service. I'm having an enjoyable time. I'm starting to laugh. And I hurt myself laughing. And God starts to move and everything and it's awesome. We get let out. And it was a little early. And somebody goes to get the vehicle. the battery's dead. So, we still ended up getting home near midnight. I want you to know God is about to do some awesome things. And we are on the verge of say verge. Because that is right on the edge. Right on the, it's like you can see it. The Promised lands there. To access. I'm telling you, these spiritual books that are in heaven right now, providing divine wisdom, knowledge, and supernatural strategy. We need it. We need strategies from the supernatural. And it's not just a little bit of wisdom. It's, it's a whole lot. It's all that is to offer, I don't want to limit what God can do in me. He's about to explode some things in you. There are some people in this room you're supposed to be authoring books. I don't care if it's a book plan. Author those books. You say oh, I want to author that book so I can get my name on it. It's not about the name either. I remember one little lady one time she authored a book many years ago and I don't even remember what the title boasts do with prayer and she gave one to me she goes that's my book. I go Where's your name at? She goes you find it ran run that book and not couldn't find her name anywhere and I go Where's your name on that book? She goes and I'm like where is that? Where's your name? How's it almost getting upset? I thought she just ignored me. She goes in there she goes turn the page something not turned to it, and she goes she that right there. I go What? She goes child of God. That's my name.

Praise God. Sometimes we try to promote ourselves. But guess what? We're supposed to promote the king. I'm not saying we can't put our name on the book. I'm not saying that in any way because there's nothing wrong with that the books that I've written that were stolen from me praise God the hammer names on them I don't know how they're going to get my name is off, but they have them. But I'm saying God it's okay to put your names on but I'm just saying we need to behave a right heart and understand what God's about to do he's about to give you such abilities to where you can see on the inner man see the heart see what's going on in their heart see that they've been hurt that they've been wounded see that people that need neither bones mended you'll be able to see the very arteries and ligaments and everything else. And I'm telling you we're about to have that supernatural ability to see come up just to be able to go into somebody and just tap their ear in there and open up supernatural miracles are going to take place and I even believe in the area of signs and wonders in the area manner are going to be restored to the church, right in the service. imagine just starts coming down. You say oh that's impossible. I want you to know of man it can come from this guy can come from a ceiling. Do you say what if it falls on the floor? I don't care if it falls in the dirt. If it's manna from heaven I am going to eat it, you say okay happen, I will tell you, you stop limiting God? Yes, get him out of the box, it's like, you know, you may find that old crackerjack box. Pop goes the weasel. get that wine god up let him pop out. And I'm not calling God a weasel. I'm just saying why don't you come up and get him out? Let him have his way. full-blown pro release, do whatever you want to do God remember in the beginning when signs of Wonder started showing up in my life. I was like, I don't know about this stuff. I don't know about this stuff. And then all of a sudden, I begin to realize that what if it's God? What if that stuff is God? Alright, God evident you have your way. You can do it. You have the full release, do whatever you want. And when I said that, lookout. He began to do all kinds of things. And you know, I have seen church after church after church begins to get hit with signs and wonders. And because the congregation has tried to diagnose, figure out dissect what is just took place. And guess what happens? There are no more signs and wonders. There are places I can just name a respectable number of places. After they've been on our services. They went through their church they had signs and wonders and guess what the church talked them out of having them well, a child's thing came apart You know, somebody lost the rings out of there, you know, lost the jewels out of the rings, that many I mean, I mean, that's what they started trying to figure it out. And guess what the Spirit of God gets grieved very easily. But at the same time, then there are other churches that I know about.

They get to specs on their hand, and they freak out. Who sides are wonders of miracles here? And that's one thing I kept telling people when we started to have a couple of specs on like, when it comes, we're gonna know. You're not gonna have to say, I see it if I hold my hand, right? You got to know it's there. Some people don't even believe it. But how many were anybody in this room at the spontaneous worship services we had at the revival? Laurie, and Tabitha, Stacy, and Brenda Yeah. Yes. Yes. But long before it came, yes. And then but it was in the service and the services or spontaneous services and ever times I'd be covered from head to toe. I'm in cover you could see me anymore. I mean, I was covered. It was thick all over me. I'd get hit and hit and hit and hit over and over and over again. You know, I just get up and boom hit again. And people could see it flying in the air. And you know, those same people that saw it flying in the air and fall have the same people that are saying it was never real? You know, nonbelief will come into you and another takeover. It will destroy you. I had to pop in me. Yes, that's funny. Strange. I have seen so much. You can never put your finger on everything. Because what about the gold fillings? What about all the different things that happen in people's bodies and, and different things that supernaturally that nobody can explain? And what about happening in people's homes? See what's getting ready happened in the days ahead is not just going to happen under one roof. It's going to happen under many roofs, people go home and find it at home. supernatural encounters are going to take place. I don't believe we have to limit it to one sanctuary. Or one motel or hotel. Come up. Even Joanie tonight. She said you're going to need a bigger room, much bigger. Springfield. I'm like now I understand. We were in the midst of a revival. Listen to me, was in the midst of a revival. And we come to Springfield. We had a couple of services left. And I preached about the glory of God at the remodel limited north. And that was one of the data services I've ever had. People I feel the service goes what's the glory I don't understand what you just preached. That doesn't make sense to me. And all these years later, I come back here, man, it's like you are eating it up now. That's like who are you now? And God keeps telling me that he's gonna break out revival in Litchfield. We're gonna have revival again in Litchfield, but I guess we're gonna have a sidetrack. I believe in the days ahead, there's gonna be people of carriers of revival, they're going to go into dead places and resurrect. I don't want to keep going because we got some things to do tonight, we're gonna minister and sometimes I got to take care of something really quick. I'm going to play a song. I want you to press into God a little bit during the song. And I'll be right back. I'm going to press in just a little bit. And we press in a little bit in unity, and then I'm going to come back and minister we're going to let God have his way. Are you ready?

Don't miss out!

Visit the website below and you can sign up to receive emails whenever Bill Vincent publishes a new book. There's no charge and no obligation.

https://books2read.com/r/B-A-XHBC-SPVSB

BOOKS 2 READ

Connecting independent readers to independent writers.

Also by Bill Vincent

Building a Prototype Church: Divine Strategies Released
Experience God's Love: By Revival Waves of Glory School of the Supernatural
Glory: Expanding God's Presence
Glory: Increasing God's Presence
Glory: Kingdom Presence of God
Glory: Pursuing God's Presence
Glory: Revival Presence of God
Rapture Revelations: Jesus Is Coming
The Prototype Church: Heaven's Strategies for Today's Church
The Secret Place of God's Power
Transitioning Into a Prototype Church: New Church Arising
Spiritual Warfare Made Simple
Aligning With God's Promises
A Closer Relationship With God
Armed for Battle: Spiritual Warfare Battle Commands
Breakthrough of Spiritual Strongholds
Desperate for God's Presence: Understanding Supernatural Atmospheres
Destroying the Jezebel Spirit: How to Overcome the Spirit Before It Destroys You!
Discerning Your Call of God
Glory: Expanding God's Presence: Discover How to Manifest God's Glory

Glory: Kingdom Presence Of God: Secrets to Becoming Ambassadors of Christ
Satan's Open Doors: Access Denied
Spiritual Warfare: The Complete Collection
The War for Spiritual Battles: Identify Satan's Strategies
Understanding Heaven's Court System: Explosive Life Changing Secrets
A Godly Shaking: Don't Create Waves
Faith: A Connection of God's Power
Global Warning: Prophetic Details Revealed
Overcoming Obstacles
Spiritual Leadership: Kingdom Foundation Principles
Glory: Revival Presence of God: Discover How to Release Revival Glory
Increasing Your Prophetic Gift: Developing a Pure Prophetic Flow
Millions of Churches: Why Is the World Going to Hell?
The Supernatural Realm: Discover Heaven's Secrets
The Unsearchable Riches of Christ: Chosen to be Sons of God
Deep Hunger: God Will Change Your Appetite Toward Him
Defeating the Demonic Realm
Glory: Increasing God's Presence: Discover New Waves of God's Glory
Growing In the Prophetic: Developing a Prophetic Voice
Healing After Divorce: Grace, Mercy and Remarriage
Love is Waiting
Awakening of Miracles: Personal Testimonies of God's Healing Power
Deception and Consequences Revealed: You Shall Know the Truth and the Truth Shall Set You Free
Overcoming the Power of Lust
Are You a Follower of Christ: Discover True Salvation
Cover Up and Save Yourself: Revealing Sexy is Not Sexy
Heaven's Court System: Bringing Justice for All
The Angry Fighter's Story: Harness the Fire Within
The Wrestler: The Pursuit of a Dream

Beginning the Courts of Heaven: Understanding the Basics
Breaking Curses: Legal Rights in the Courts of Heaven
Writing and Publishing a Book: Secrets of a Christian Author
How to Write a Book: Step by Step Guide
The Anointing: Fresh Oil of God's Presence
Spiritual Leadership: Kingdom Foundation Principles Second Edition
The Courts of Heaven: How to Present Your Case
The Jezebel Spirit: Tactics of Jezebel's Control
Heaven's Angels: The Nature and Ranking of Angels
Don't Know What to Do?: Discover Promotion in the Wilderness
Word of the Lord: Prophetic Word for 2020
The Coronavirus Prophecy
Increase Your Anointing: Discover the Supernatural
Apostolic Breakthrough: Birthing God's Purposes
The Healing Power of God: Releasing the Power of the Holy Spirit
The Secret Place of God's Power: Revelations of God's Word
The Rapture: Details of the Second Coming of Christ
Increase of Revelation and Restoration: Reveal, Recover & Restore
Leadership vs Management
Restoration of the Soul: The Presence of God Changes Everything
Building a Prototype Church: The Church is in a Season of Profound of Change
Keys to Receiving Your Miracle: Miracles Happen Today
The Resurrection Power of God: Great Exploits of God
Transitioning to the Prototype Church: The Church is in a Season of Profound of Transition
Waves of Revival: Expect the Unexpected
The Stronghold of Jezebel: A True Story of a Man's Journey
Glory: Pursuing God's Presence: Revealing Secrets
Like a Mighty Rushing Wind
Steps to Revival
Supernatural Power

Watch for more at https://revivalwavesofgloryministries.com/.

About the Author

Bill Vincent is no stranger to understanding the power of God. Not only has he spent over twenty years as a Minister with a strong prophetic anointing, he is now also an Apostle and Author with Revival Waves of Glory Ministries in Litchfield, IL. Along with his wife, Tabitha, he, leads a team providing apostolic oversight in all aspects of ministry, including service, personal ministry and Godly character.

Bill offers a wide range of writings and teachings from deliverance, to experiencing presence of God and developing Apostolic cutting edge Church structure. Drawing on the power of the Holy Spirit through years of experience in Revival, Spiritual Sensitivity, and deliverance ministry, Bill now focuses mainly on pursuing the Presence of God and breaking the power of the devil off of people's lives.

His books 50 and counting has since helped many people to overcome the spirits and curses of Satan. For more information or to keep up with Bill's latest releases, please visit www.revivalwavesofgloryministries.com. To contact Bill, feel free to follow him on twitter @revivalwaves.

Read more at https://revivalwavesofgloryministries.com/.

About the Publisher

Accepting manuscripts in the most categories. We love to help people get their words available to the world.

Revival Waves of Glory focus is to provide more options to be published. We do traditional paperbacks, hardcovers, audio books and ebooks all over the world. A traditional royalty-based publisher that offers self-publishing options, Revival Waves provides a very author friendly and transparent publishing process, with President Bill Vincent involved in the full process of your book. Send us your manuscript and we will contact you as soon as possible.

Contact: Bill Vincent at rwgpublishing@yahoo.com www.rwgpublishing.com

www.ingramcontent.com/pod-product-compliance
Lightning Source LLC
LaVergne TN
LVHW042004060526
838200LV00041B/1875